Motivational Quotes Book

200 Inspirational, Self-Help, Mindfulness and Powerful Quotes

Dr SAJEEV M S

COPYRIGHT

Copyright © 2023 Dr SAJEEV M S

All rights reserved

The characters and events portrayed in this book are fictitious. Any similarity to real persons, living or dead, is coincidental and not intended by the author.

No part of this book may be reproduced, or stored in a retrieval system, or transmitted in any form or by any means, electronic, mechanical, photocopying, recording, or otherwise, without express written permission of the publisher.

ABOUT THE AUTHOR

Dr.Sajeev.M.S is an eminent educator in India with two decades of experience in the field of education. Alongside his role as an educator, he is a Certified Soft-Skills Trainer, a Certified School Counselor, Accredited Teacher Trainer, Motivator, Writer and Author.

He holds the position of Executive Advisor and Fellow Member of The International Association of Educators and Corporate Trainers (IAECT) as well as a Fellow Member of Edoxia Research University, USA. He is a Lifetime Member of The International Association of Soft-Skills Trainers (IAST) and the Chairman of the Global Advisory Board for Emerald Edu-Concept and Services, Nigeria.

He has received over 20 National and International Awards and recognitions for his exemplary work and sincere efforts in the field of education. They include 'Global Best Role Model Award 2021', Educational Leader of the Year Award', Best Management Leader Award', 'Excellence in Academics Award', Best Teacher Award', Best Achiever's Award', 'International Educational Ambassador Award', and APJ Abdul Kalam Award' 'Best Educator Award 2023' 'Edu Leader Award-2023' 'Global Best Mentor Award'

Learning is his passion. It never ends...... His successful journey continues......

TABLE OF CONTENTS

INTRODUCTION

This 'Inspirational Quotes Book.' goes beyond the commonplace, providing a comprehensive investigation of the human spirit via carefully chosen and inspirational statements. From renowned intellectuals' insightful insights to the timeless wisdom of unknown voices, each quote embodies the essence of perseverance, optimism, and resolve. This book is divided into 12 strong chapters, each containing lots of inspirational quotes. It will drastically alter your life and career. This book is more than just a collection of words; it is a guide to realizing your entire potential. These statements act as beacons of light, guiding you through the complexity of existence, whether you seek motivation for personal growth, career success, or managing life's problems. Allow each page to serve as a source of inspiration, a reminder of your inner strength, and a catalyst for positive change. The 'Inspirational Quotes Book' is your daily companion on your journey to a more inspired and fulfilling life.

CHAPTER: 1

The Power of Positivity

A positive mindset is characterized by an optimistic, hopeful, and constructive mental attitude

<u>Positive Thinking</u>

"Positivity is a choice. When you choose positive thoughts, you create a positive life."

- Unknown

*****

"Your mind is a powerful thing. When you fill it with positive thoughts, your life will start to change."

- Unknown

******

"Positive thinking will let you do everything better than negative thinking will."

- Zig Ziglar

******

"The only limit to our realization of tomorrow will be our doubts of today"

- Franklin D. Roosevelt

******

"Your attitude determines your direction."

- John C. Maxwell

******

"Positive thinking is more than just a tagline. It changes the way we behave. And I firmly believe that when I am positive, it not only makes me better, but it also makes those around me better."

- Harvey

******

Mackay"Believe you can and you're halfway there."

-Theodore Roosevelt

******

"The pessimist complains about the wind; the optimist expects it to change; the realist adjusts the sails."

- William Arthur Ward

******

"Positive thinking is not about expecting the best to happen every time but accepting that whatever happens is the best for this moment"

Unknown

******

"Positive thinking is empowering; it pushes you to take action, to make things happen, to turn dreams into reality."

- Dr. T.P. Chia

******

<u>Positive Mindset</u>

"Train your mind to see the good in every situation. A positive mindset is the fuel for resilience and growth."

- Marie Forleo

******

"Positivity is not just a state of mind; it's a way of life. Choose it daily, and watch how it transforms your world."

- Lewis Howes

*****

"A positive mindset can turn a setback into a comeback."

-Chante Dy

******

"Your thoughts shape your reality. Choose positivity, and you'll attract a world of possibilities."

- Annette White

******

"Optimism is the faith that leads to achievement. Cultivate a positive mindset, and you'll find the strength to overcome any obstacle."

- Helen Keller

******

"A positive mindset sees opportunities in every challenge. It's not about denying difficulties but choosing to focus on solutions."

- Tony Robbins

****

"Your mindset is the architect of your success. Design it with positivity, and your life will be a masterpiece."

- Shiv Khera

****

"In the midst of challenges, maintain a positive mindset. It's the key to unlocking solutions and discovering your inner strength."

- Diane Gottsman

****

"Positivity is a magnet for miracles. Keep your mindset bright, and watch the extraordinary unfold."

- Marla Gibbs

****

"The most powerful tool you have is your mind. Cultivate a positive mindset, and you'll cultivate a life of limitless possibilities."

- Jay Shett

****

CHAPTER: 2

Gratitude and Mindfulness

Mindfulness is a mental state characterized by a focused and non-judgmental awareness of the present moment

<u>Gratitude</u>

"Gratitude is when memory is stored in the heart and not in the mind."

- Lionel Hampton

****

"Gratitude is the sweetest thing in a seeker's life – in all human life. If there is gratitude in your heart, then there will be tremendous sweetness in your eyes."

- Sri Chinmoy

****

"Gratitude is the inward feeling of kindness received. Thankfulness is the natural impulse to express that feeling. Thanksgiving is the following of that impulse."

- Henry Van Dyke

****

"Gratitude can transform common days into thanksgivings, turn routine jobs into joy, and change ordinary opportunities into blessings."

- William Arthur Ward

*****

"Gratitude makes sense of our past, brings peace for today, and creates a vision for tomorrow."

- Melody Beattie

*****

"Gratitude is the healthiest of all human emotions. The more you express gratitude for what you have, the more likely you will have even more to express gratitude for."

- Zig Ziglar

******

"Gratitude turns what we have into enough."

- Aesop

*****

"Gratitude is not only the greatest of virtues but the parent of all others."

- Marcus Tullius Cicero

*****

"Gratitude makes sense of our past, brings peace for today, and creates a vision for tomorrow."

- Melody Beattie

*****

"Gratitude is the fairest blossom which springs from the soul."

- Henry Ward Beecher

*****

Mindfulness

"Mindfulness isn't difficult, we just need to remember to do it."

- Sharon Salzberg

*****

"Mindfulness is the key to unlock the fullness of life. It's how we become fully present, fully engaged in the here and now."

******

- Deepak Chopra"The present moment is the only moment available to us, and it is the door to all moments."

- Thich Nhat Hanh

*****

"Mindfulness is about love and loving life. When you cultivate this love, it gives you clarity and compassion for life, and your actions happen in accordance with that."

- Jon Kabat-Zinn

*****

"Mindfulness is the aware, balanced acceptance of the present experience. It isn't more complicated than that. It is opening to or receiving the present moment, pleasant or unpleasant, just as it is, without either clinging to it or rejecting it."

- Sylvia Boorstein

******

"The best way to capture moments is to pay attention. This is how we cultivate mindfulness."

- Jon Kabat-Zinn

******

"Mindfulness is simply being aware of what is happening right now without wishing it were different; enjoying the pleasant without holding on when it changes (which it will); being with the unpleasant without fearing it will always be this way ."

-James Baraz

"Feelings come and go like clouds in a windy sky. Conscious breathing is my anchor."

- Thich Nhat Hanh

******

"Mindfulness is the direct path to freedom, and it is the gentle effort to be continuously present with experience."

- Jack Kornfield

******

"Mindfulness is the quality and power of mind that is aware of what's happening—without commentary and without interference."

- Sharon Salzberg

******

CHAPTER: 3

Resilience and Overcoming Challenges

Overcome Challenges

"Success is not final, failure is not fatal: It is the courage to continue that counts."

- Winston S. Churchill

*****

"In the middle of difficulty lies opportunity."

- Albert Einstein

******

"The only way to achieve the impossible is to believe it is possible."

- Charles Kingsleigh (from Alice in Wonderland)

******

"It's not whether you get knocked down, it's whether you get up."

- Vince Lombardi

"Challenges are what make life interesting. Overcoming them is what makes life meaningful."

- Joshua J. Marine

******

"Strength does not come from the body. It comes from the will."

- Arnold Schwarzenegger

*****

"Your attitude, not your aptitude, will determine your altitude."

- Zig Ziglar

******

"Obstacles don't have to stop you. If you run into a wall, don't turn around and give up. Figure out how to climb it, go through it, or work around it."

- Michael Jordan

*****

"Every adversity, every failure, every heartache carries with it the seed of an equal or greater benefit."

- Napoleon Hill

******

"Our greatest glory is not in never falling, but in rising every time we fall."

– Confucius

******

Resilience

"The greatest glory in living lies not in never falling, but in rising every time we fall."

- Nelson Mandela

******

"Do not judge me by my success, judge me by how many times I fell down and got back up again."

Nelson Mandela

******

"You have within you right now, everything you need to deal with whatever the world can throw at you."

- Brian Tracy

******

"Resilience is not what happens to you. It's how you react to, respond to, and recover from what happens to you."

- Dr. Rick Hanson

"You may not control all the events that happen to you, but you can decide not to be reduced by them."

- Maya Angelou

******

"Resilience is accepting your new reality, even if it's less good than the one you had before."

- Elizabeth Edwards

******

"It's not that I'm so smart, it's just that I stay with problems longer."

- Albert Einstein

****

"The human capacity for burden is like bamboo – far more flexible than you'd ever believe at first glance."

- Jodi Picoult

****

"The oak fought the wind and was broken, the willow bent when it must and survived."

- Robert Jordan

******

"Life doesn't get easier or more forgiving; we get stronger and more resilient."

- Steve Maraboli

****

CHAPTER: 4

Kindness and Compassion

Kindness

"Kindness in words creates confidence. Kindness in thinking creates profoundness. Kindness in giving creates love."

- Lao Tzu

******

"Carry out a random act of kindness, with no expectation of reward, safe in the knowledge that one day someone might do the same for you."

- Princess Diana

****

"Be kind whenever possible. It is always possible."

- Dalai Lama

******

"Kindness is the language which the deaf can hear and the blind can see."

- Mark Twain

"No act of kindness, no matter how small, is ever wasted."

- Aesop

"Kindness is the sunshine in which virtue grows."

- Robert Green Ingersoll

******

"Kind words can be short and easy to speak, but their echoes are truly endless."

- Mother Teresa

****

In a world where you can be anything, be kind."

- Jennifer Dukes Lee

******

"Kindness is the ability to know what the right thing to do is and having the courage to do it."

- R.A.Kishi

****

"Too often we underestimate the power of a touch, a smile, a kind word, a listening ear, an honest compliment, or the smallest act of caring, all of which have the potential to turn a life around."

- Leo Buscaglia

****

Compassion

"Our task must be to free ourselves by widening our circle of compassion to embrace all living creatures and the whole of nature and its beauty."

Albert Einstein

******

"Compassion is the radicalism of our time."

- Dalai Lama

******

"When we give cheerfully and accept gratefully, everyone is blessed."

- Maya Angelou

****

"Compassion is the foundation of everything positive, very thing good. If you carry the power of compassion to the marketplace and the dinner table, you can make your life really count."

- R.A. Salvatore

******

"Compassion is the keen awareness of the interdependence of all things."

- Thomas Merton

******

"To keep a lamp burning, we have to keep putting oil in it."

- Mother Teresa

******

"Compassion brings us to a stop, and for a moment we rise above ourselves."

- Mason Cooley

****

"Compassion is not a relationship between the healer and the wounded. It's a relationship between equals."

- Pema Chödrön

******

"The simplest acts of kindness are by far more powerful than a thousand heads bowing in prayer."

- Mahatma Gandhi

****

"If you want others to be happy, practice compassion. If you want to be happy, practice compassion."

- Dalai Lama

******

CHAPTER: 5

Pursuing Passion

"Embrace your passion like Maya, for it is the poetry of your soul waiting to be written."

- Maya Angelou

******

"Follow your passion fearlessly, for as Eleanor Roosevelt once said, 'The future belongs to those who believe in the beauty of their dreams.'"

- Eleanor Roosevelt

****

"In the pursuit of passion, channel the audacity of Steve Jobs and innovate your way to greatness."

–Steve Jobs

"Let your passion be the symphony of your life, echoing the melody of your heart. Beethoven would be proud."

- Ludwig van Beethoven

******

As Albert Einstein wisely noted, 'Imagination is more important than knowledge.' In your pursuit of passion, let your imagination be your guiding star."

- Albert Einstein

"Passion is the engine that drives success, as Henry Ford once envisioned. Start your engines and journey toward your dreams."

- Henry Ford

******

"Audrey Hepburn's grace and passion remind us that elegance is the perfect accessory to a life lived with purpose and passion."

- Audrey Hepburn

******

"Passion is the canvas on which you paint the masterpiece of your life. Channel your inner Picasso and create with bold strokes."

- Pablo Picasso

******

"In the words of Oprah Winfrey, 'Passion is energy. Feel the power that comes from focusing on what excites you.' Let your passion energize your journey."

- Oprah Winfrey

******

"Walt Disney believed, 'All our dreams can come true if we have the courage to pursue them.' Be courageous in pursuing your passion; your dreams are waiting."

- Walt Disney

*****

CHAPTER: 6

Persistence and Hard Work

Persistence

"The difference between a successful person and others is not a lack of strength, not a lack of knowledge, but rather a lack in will."

- Vince Lombardi

******

"The only guarantee for failure is to stop trying."

- John C. Maxwell

****

"I do know one thing about me: I don't measure myself by others' expectations or let others define my worth."

- Sonia Sotomayor

*****

"The difference between a successful person and others is not a lack of strength, not a lack of knowledge, but rather a lack of will."

- Vince Lombardi

"Our greatest glory is not in never falling, but in rising every time we fall."

- Confucius

******

"Success is not final, failure is not fatal: It is the courage to continue that counts."

- Winston Churchill

******

"Perseverance is not a long race; it's many short races one after another."

- Walter Elliot

******

"It's not that I'm so smart, it's just that I stay with problems longer."

- Albert Einstein

******

"I do not think there is any other quality so essential to success of any kind as the quality of perseverance. It overcomes almost everything, even nature."

- John D. Rockefeller

******

"Persistence can change failure into extraordinary achievement."

- Matt Biondi

Hard Work

"The dictionary is the only place that success comes before work, work is the key to success, and hard work can help you accomplish anything."

- Vince Lombardi

******

"I find that the harder I work, the more luck I seem to have."

- Thomas Jefferson

******

"There is no substitute for hard work."

- Thomas Edison

******

"I'm a great believer in luck, and I find the harder I work, the more I have of it."

- Thomas Jefferson

******

"Success is built sequentially. It's one thing at a time."

- Gary Keller

****

"Success is no accident. It is hard work, perseverance, learning, studying, sacrifice, and most of all, love of what you are doing or learning to do."

- Pelé

"The only place where success comes before work is in the dictionary."

- Vidal Sassoon

******

"Hard work spotlights the character of people: some turn up their sleeves, some turn up their noses, and some don't turn up at all."

- Sam Ewing

******

"I never dreamed about success. I worked for it."

- Estée Lauder

******

"Hard work beats talent when talent doesn't work hard."

- Tim Notke

******

CHAPTER: 7

Self-Discovery and Growth

Self-Discovery

"To find yourself, think for yourself."

- Socrates

****

"The only journey is the one within."

- Rainer Maria Rilke

****

"The greatest adventure is not in seeking new landscapes, but in having new eyes."

- Marcel Proust

******

"Knowing yourself is the beginning of all wisdom."

- Aristotle

****

"The most important journey you will take in your life will usually be the one of self-transformation."

- Shannon L. Alder

******

"The privilege of a lifetime is to become who you truly are."

- Carl Jung

*****

"Don't spend your life trying to impress others. Be yourself, live your own life, and don't ever apologize for it."

- Lee Iacocca

******

"Your task is not to seek for love, but merely to seek and find all the barriers within yourself that you have built against it."

- Rumi

"Your time is limited, don't waste it living someone else's life."

- Steve Jobs

******

"The more you know yourself, the more you understand life, the more you value your time."

- Maxime Lagacé

******

Growth

"Personal development is a major time-saver. The better you become, the less time it takes you to achieve your goals."

- Brian Tracy

****

"The only person you are destined to become is the person you decide to be."

- Ralph Waldo Emerson

******

"The greatest investment you can make is in yourself."

- Warren Buffett

******

"Your life does not get better by chance, it gets better by change."

- Jim Rohn

*****

"The purpose of learning is growth, and our minds, unlike our bodies, can continue growing as we continue to live."

- Mortimer Adler

******

"Change is the end result of all true learning."

- Leo Buscaglia

"If you want to achieve greatness, stop asking for permission."

- Anonymous

******

"Invest in yourself, and your dreams. Grind now, shine later."

- Anonymous

****

"The only limit to our realization of tomorrow will be our doubts of today."

- Franklin D. Roosevelt

******

"The only way to do great work is to love what you do."

- Steve Jobs

******

CHAPTER: 8

Embracing Change

"Change is the end result of all true learning."

- Leo Buscaglia

******

"Change is hard at first, messy in the middle, and gorgeous at the end."

- Robin Sharma

******

"When we are no longer able to change a situation, we are challenged to change ourselves."

- Viktor E. Frankl

******

"The only way to make sense out of change is to plunge into it, move with it, and join the dance."

- Alan Watts

****

"Change is the law of life. And those who look only to the past or the present are certain to miss the future."

- John F. Kennedy

******

"Embrace uncertainty. Some of the most beautiful chapters in our lives won't have a title until much later."

- Bob Goff

****

"Change is not only likely, it's inevitable."

- Barbara Sher

******

"Your life does not get better by chance, it gets better by change."

- Jim Rohn

"Change your life today. Don't gamble on the future; act now, without delay."

- Simone de Beauvoir

******

"The world as we have created it is a process of our thinking. It cannot be changed without changing our thinking."

- Albert Einstein

******

CHAPTER: 9

Courage and Taking Risks

Courage

"Courage is resistance to fear, mastery of fear—not the absence of fear."

- Mark Twain

******

"You gain strength, courage, and confidence by every experience in which you really stop to look fear in the face."

- Eleanor Roosevelt

*****

"Success is not final, failure is not fatal: It is the courage to continue that counts."

- Winston Churchill

******

"Courage is not the absence of fear, but rather the assessment that something else is more important than fear."

- Franklin D. Roosevelt

******

"Have the courage to follow your heart and intuition. They somehow know what you truly want to become."

- Steve Jobs

******

"Courage is what it takes to stand up and speak. Courage is also what it takes to sit down and listen."

- Winston Churchill

******

"It takes courage to grow up and become who you really are."

- E.E. Cummings

****

"Courage is not simply one of the virtues but the form of every virtue at the testing point."

- C.S. Lewis

******

"The only limit to our realization of tomorrow will be our doubts of today."

- Franklin D. Roosevelt

******

"It takes a great deal of bravery to stand up to our enemies, but just as much to stand up to our friends."

- J.K. Rowling

******

Taking Risks

"Life is either a daring adventure or nothing at all."

- Helen Keller

******

"It's not whether you get knocked down, it's whether you get up."

- Vince Lombardi

******

"If you are not willing to risk the usual, you will have to settle for the ordinary."

- Jim Rohn

******

"Don't be afraid to give up the good to go for the great."

- John D. Rockefeller

******

"The biggest risk is not taking any risk. In a world that's changing really quickly, the only strategy that is guaranteed to fail is not taking risks."

- Mark Zuckerberg

*****

"Security is mostly a superstition. Life is either a daring adventure or nothing."

- Helen Keller

"Only those who will risk going too far can possibly find out how far one can go."

- T.S. Eliot

******

"Do not be embarrassed by your failures, learn from them and start again."

- Richard Branson

******

"Take risks: if you win, you will be happy; if you lose, you will be wise."

- Anonymous

*****

"The only way to do great work is to love what you do. If ou haven't found it yet, keep looking. Don't settle."

- Steve Jobs

CHAPTER: 10

Career Success

"Your career is like a garden. It requires careful cultivation, hard work, and dedication. But with patience and persistence, it will bloom into something beautiful."

- Oprah Winfrey

******

"Success is not measured by the position one has reached in life but by the obstacles which he has overcome."

- Booker T. Washington

******

Choose a job you love, and you will never have to work a day in your life."

- Confucius

******

"Your work is going to fill a large part of your life, and the only way to be truly satisfied is to do what you believe is great work. And the only way to do great work is to love what you do."

- Steve Jobs

****

"Success is liking yourself, liking what you do, and liking how you do it."

- Maya Angelou

******

"Success is not just about climbing up the corporate ladder; it's about making a meaningful impact on the lives of others."

- Michelle Obama

******

"Don't be afraid to give up the good to go for the great."

- John D. Rockefeller

*****

"Success is not final, failure is not fatal: It is the courage to continue that counts."

- Winston Churchill

******

"The future belongs to those who believe in the beauty of their dreams."

- Eleanor Roosevelt

******

"Your career is a journey, not a destination. Enjoy the process, embrace the challenges, and celebrate every milestone along the way."

- Tony Robbin

****

CHAPTER: 11

Time Management

"Time is what we want most, but what we use worst."

- William Penn

****

"The way we spend our time defines who we are."

- Jonathan Estrin

****

"Your time is limited, don't waste it living someone else's life."

- Steve Jobs

****

"Time is a created thing. To say 'I don't have time,' is like saying, 'I don't want to.'"

- Lao Tzu

****

"The best time to plant a tree was 20 years ago. The second best time is now."

- *Chinese Proverb*

******

"Time is a great teacher, but unfortunately it kills all its pupils."

- *Louis Hector Berlioz*

******

"The key is in not spending time, but in investing it."

- *Stephen R. Covey*

"Don't be fooled by the calendar. There are only as many days in the year as you make use of."

- *Charles Richards*

******

Time isn't the main thing. It's the only thing."

- *Miles Davis*

*****

"The common man is not concerned about the passage of time, the man of talent is driven by it."

- *Shoppenhauer*

****

CHAPTER: 12

Punctuality

"Punctuality is the art of guessing how late the other fellow is going to be."

- Evelyn Waugh

******

"Punctuality is the soul of business."

- Thomas Chandler Haliburton

******

"Punctuality is not just limited to arriving at a place at right time; it is also about taking actions at right time."

- Amit Kalantri

****

"Punctuality is the virtue of the bored."

- Evelyn Waugh

****

"Punctuality is not just limited to arriving at a place at right time; it is also about taking actions at right time."

- Amit Kalantri

"I could never think well of a man's intellectual or moral character if he was habitually unfaithful to his appointments."

- Nathaniel Emmons

******

"Punctuality is the politeness of kings."

- Louis XVIII

****

"The trouble with being punctual is that nobody's there to appreciate it."

- Franklin P. Jones

******

"The best way to ensure that others respect your time is to always respect theirs."

- Russell Clayton

*****

"Punctuality is the thief of time."

- Oscar Wilde

******

CONCLUSION

As we near the end of the 'Motivational Quotes Book,' consider this more than a conclusion—consider it an invitation to weave the transformative power of these words into the fabric of your daily life. The trip through these inspiring quotes is not designed to be a one-time event, but rather a continuous source of motivation. Take the wisdom that spoke to you from this book, the encouragement that ignited your spirit, and the reminders of your inner power with you.

May these quotes serve as beacons of light in times of darkness, catalysts for progress in times of stagnation, and continuous companions on your journey to live a meaningful and purposeful life! You may remember that the genuine power of inspiration is found in the acts that are inspired rather than the words themselves. You should accept the lessons, nurture resilience, and allow the echoes of these quotes to propel you into a future filled with purpose, passion, and the unyielding belief that you have the power to design your own destiny. Your adventure has only just begun; let these quotes serve as the wind beneath your wings. Continue your successful journey.

Best wishes to all readers.

www.ingramcontent.com/pod-product-compliance
Lightning Source LLC
Chambersburg PA
CBHW070815280726
48660CB00015B/949